Greater Than a Tourist - Paris France

50 Travel Tips from a Local

Albane Linyer

Order Information: To order this title please email lbrenenc@gmail.com or visit GreaterThanATourist.com. A bulk discount can be provided.

Cover Template Creator: Lisa Rusczyk Ed. D. using Canva.
Cover Creator: Lisa Rusczyk Ed. D.
Image: https://pixabay.com/en/paris-france-city-urban-sky-1804483/

Lock Haven, PA
ISBN: 9781549722899

>TOURIST

Albane Linyer

BOOK DESCRIPTION

Are you excited about planning your next trip?

Do you want to try something new?

Would you like some guidance from a local?

If you answered yes to any of these questions, then this Greater Than a Tourist book is for you.

Greater Than a Tourist by Albane Linyer offers the inside scoop on Paris. Most travel books tell you how to sightsee. Although there's nothing wrong with that, as a part of the Greater than a Tourist series, this book will give you tips from someone who lives at your next travel destination. In these pages, you'll discover local advice that will help you throughout your trip.

Travel like a local. Slow down and get to know the people and the culture of a place. By the time you finish this book, you will be eager and prepared to travel to your next destination.

Albane Linyer

TABLE OF CONTENTS

Albane Linyer

Our Story

Notes

DEDICATION

This book is dedicated to Madeleine, with whom I discovered Paris and been to Le Marais for the first time. To Caroline, who showed what a wonderful playground Paris is. To Adele, who made this city feel like home.

Albane Linyer

2

ABOUT THE AUTHOR

Albane is a London-based writer and screenwriter. She was born in Paris, then moved to Moscow as a child. A few years later, she came back to live in Paris. Eager to discover more and travel the world, she moved to Lisbon on an exchange program. She now lives in London, where she graduated in Dramatic Writing from the University of Arts. In spite of living in the UK, Albane still considers Paris as home and is back there very often.

Albane loves travelling and even more experiencing life in different cities. She is also passionate about languages and speaks fluent French, English and Russian, and a little bit of Portuguese.

In every city I go, I try to find the small restaurants, the local bars that you will not find in any touristic guide. Thanks to my family, my friends and years spent living in the city, Paris has opened many secrets to me. It is now the time to share some with you!

Albane Linyer

HOW TO USE THIS BOOK

The Greater Than a Tourist book series was written by someone who has lived in an area for over three months. The goal of this book is to help travelers either dream or experience different locations by providing opinions from a local. The author has made suggestions based on their own experiences. Please do your own research before traveling to the area in case the suggested places are unavailable.

Albane Linyer

FROM THE PUBLISHER

Traveling can be one of the most important parts of a person's life. The anticipation and memories that you have are some of the best. As a publisher of the Greater Than a Tourist book series, as well as the popular 50 Things to Know book series, we strive to help you learn about new places, spark your imagination, and inspire you. Wherever you are and whatever you do I wish you safe, fun, and inspiring travel.

Lisa Rusczyk Ed. D.

CZYK Publishing

Albane Linyer

WELCOME TO > TOURIST

Albane Linyer

INTRODUCTION

Paris is in the **top three cities in the world** that attract the
most tourists. You can fear that you will be a drop in the rain,
trying to get a glimpse of the Eiffel Tower and coming back
home having seen mostly other tourists. It won't be the case.
Even if you have not read a word about the city before
visiting it, you cannot not fall in love with the small streets of
Le Marais, the sunsets on the Seine when the city is bright
pink, the countless shopping temptations and above all – the
food.

Paris has remained an authentic city, and Parisian people are
way nicer than what you would expect from their reputation.
Whether you like to walk, cycle, dance, eat, drink or just be
surrounded by art, there is a place – and more than one I am
sure – in this book for you.

Albane Linyer

1. The Best Season To Book Your Trip To Paris

France changes with the seasons and so does its capital. The most important person to question before you plan your trip is yourself. What kind of atmosphere are you looking for during your stay? Summer in Paris is magical, the whole city is quiet, filled with cool ephemeral venues, but it can get quite hot and some nice places are closed. Winter can be cold but there is no better cure than a nice cup of hot chocolate and a heated terrace. Parisian spring is filled with a special energy and enthusiasm, the city is coming back to life after a winter spent cocooning. To me, the time of the year that has the most Parisian vibe is definitely autumn. It is usually not too cold and, with all the Parisians being back from holidays, you will be able to get a sense of the city's essence. Each season brings up a different side of Paris, so you are free to choose the one that suits you the best!

2. Don't Get The "Paris Syndrome"

If you have never heard of it, don't panic: the Paris Syndrome is not a real disease that you might catch walking next to the Seine. The expression designates the disappointment of tourists who come to Paris believing that they will find Parisians wearing a beret and carrying a baguette under their arm at every corner.

Not being disappointed by your trip is all about what you expect from it. If you only walk down the Champs-Elysées, all you will see are tourists and luxury brands. If you spend most of your days in Montmartre, you will be surrounded by adorable cafes, restaurants, and musicians in a very Parisian setting. If you go to Pigalle, be ready to live among the Parisian youth and to party all night! It is important to know what you are looking for.

Also, don't be sad: you will probably see a Parisian carrying a baguette at some point, especially if you wait long enough in front of a bakery.

3. Sentences In French Parisian People Don't Want To Hear

When you visit a foreign country, using a few words from the local language is always a plus. Parisian people love to hear "Bonjour" and "Merci", and of course the classic "Comment allez-vous?". However, it is not because you know some words in French that you should use all of them in France, especially with strangers. So please, avoid asking a French girl "Voulez-vous coucher avec moi?" if you don't know her. It might not be your mother tongue, but it is still rude. Also, stating that "J'adore Moulin Rouge!" is not the best conversation opener, because most of us have never been there.

Here are a few sentences that will impress your audience rather than scare them or make them feel uncomfortable.

"Cet endroit est super" which means "This place is great!" if a French person takes you to a place they particularly like. "Je voudrais acheter du vin." "I would like to buy some wine.". That one is in case you are wondering where to buy the most French souvenir of all. Also works with "Je voudrais acheter des cigarettes/du pain" for cigarettes and bread. Finally, "Merci pour cette journée" Which is "Thank you for today" after long hours walking around the city.

4. Sentences To Approach Real Parisians In Flesh

What should you say when talking to a French person? The legend says that French people don't speak English. It might be true in other parts of the country, but Parisians love to practice their English skills and brag about it!

Here are some sentences to break the ice. The classic "Let me buy you a drink/ Do you have a lighter" is always a good idea if you are looking to make some friends on a night out. Try and find people who seem to be in the same vibe as you are and ask them where they are going later: a great technique to get to know new places and get the chance to party with local people! If you are not looking to bond that much but only to exchange a few words, ask for your direction in a shop or try to get tips about the city from a waiter. They usually know a lot about the city and will probably be happy to help you.

5. Rive Droite, Rive Gauche – Left Bank, Right Bank

As well as many other big cities, Paris is divided between its southern and its northern part. The easiest way to split our beautiful city in two was to use the river, the Seine. Here we are, Paris has a Rive Gauche – Left Bank – and a Rive Droite – Right Bank –. Traditionally, the Left Bank was said to be the intellectual part of Paris, with its elegant and sophisticated atmosphere. The Café de Flore, a symbol of the area, was famous for having Jean-Paul Sartre and Simone de Beauvoir as regular customers. Rive Droite, at the contrary, was supposed to be a bit more edgy, especially in the North. Its West was home to the French bourgeoisie. In the modern times, Right Bank became known for having many clubs and alternative venues, being loud and artistic. As to knowing if it is still true today, you are free to make up your own mind. In my opinion, Paris has become so big and diverse that each of the riversides is composed of different smaller areas and each one has its own style.

6. The Arrondissements

Arrondissements are the Parisian neighborhoods, there are twenty of them and each one is quite unique. You learn about a Parisian's personality just by asking them where they live. There is no good or bad arrondissement, however, if you are in Paris for a short time, it will be easier to stay close to the things you are interested in. Keep in mind that there can be quite a wide price range between the arrondissements, and the closer to the center, the more expensive. On a budget, rather go for an Airbnb in the 10th arrondissement than for a hotel room in the 4th. The choice of an arrondissement also depends on your personality. You want to save money, have an artistic soul and know the movie *Amelie Poulain* by heart? Go East, around the 19th arrondissement. You are a trendy foodista and willing to pay what it takes for the crème de la crème of Parisian shopping? The 2nd and the 4th arrondissement are made for you! A romantic book lover, passionate about philosophy would find themselves at home in Saint-Germain-des-Près, in the 6th. Nevertheless, if you just want to see Paris, do a bit of everything and see the most famous landmarks, I will always advise staying in the 1st arrondissement. There are some affordable places to stay and it is at the very center of the city; you will be able to get anywhere in no-time and walk to most places.

7. Take The Bus

No, Parisian buses are not as iconic as the ones in London. However, if you are in Paris for a short time, buses are a great way to get to know the city. I am not talking about sightseeing buses, just try to get from one place to another using this mean rather than the underground.

From the windows, try to spot the landmarks, but also some nice-looking streets and appealing cafes and restaurants. Reading the names of the bus stops is a good way of remembering the different places you have been to. So come aboard and let the driver show you the city while you are already thinking about that delicious "boeuf Bourguignon" you are going to have for dinner. As a piece of advice, avoid the bus on very hot days and prefer walking. Your journey will probably be more pleasant and it saves seats for elderly people who don't have a choice!

8. Velib

Velib is the mysterious word designating Paris' public bicycles. You will find stations pretty much everywhere and the rental is quite cheap if you return the bike on time. Be careful when choosing your bike, take the time to check that all the components are in working state, otherwise you might have a bad surprise after a few meters.

Paris benefits from a great network of cycle paths, which will enable you to discover the city and stop whenever you see a nice spot. Riding a bicycle is the most autonomous way to travel the city. Eastern Paris especially is quite pleasant, you can almost always come across cycle paths. On a sunny day, there is no better feeling than riding by the riverside.

This being said, be careful: Paris is a big city and the traffic requires your full attention at all times.

9. Taxi, Uber,...?

When you need to go somewhere quickly, a car is the easiest way. Still, it is hard to choose between all the options available in a big city. When Uber first became available in Paris, I would have advised you to use the app instead of taking a regular taxi, mostly to save money. However, the Uber phenomenon has had both negative and beneficial effects: the Parisian taxis are now cheaper and way more polite, while Uber rides are increasingly more expensive. In a nutshell, take whichever car is close to you.

A local tip though: there is a new little app called LeCab that offers a cheap service in inner Paris. If you have some time before leaving your room or apartment, try and compare the prices.

10. Grands Boulevards

Grands Boulevards, as its name states, is a big boulevard. Nothing special will you say, except that the place is well-known among Parisians for being home to many bars and clubs. You will always find something to do, drink, or dance on! For the techno lovers, the Rex club, one of the most worldwide famous venues for electronic music, is just seconds away. For those missing the music of the 90's and the 80's, the Memphis is also very nearby.

Grands Boulevards is also a good place to find an Irish Pub and have a Guinness. The boulevard and its clubs being highly frequented by Erasmus students, it is unlikely that people will judge you for not speaking French.

Overall, a great place for meeting people and having a couple of beers before you go clubbing. Food wise, unless it is 5 a.m and you are craving French fries and a kebab, I would advise you to go off the boulevard for a meal.

Grands Boulevards is ideally located between the trendy areas of Pigalle and the 2nd arrondissement, you cannot go wrong. Both sides offer great restaurants. In addition, Pigalle has got some touristic spots and the 2nd arrondissement is a great area to spend the day shopping and Instragraming awesome food.

To breath the air of Paris preserves the soul.

Victor Hugo

Albane Linyer

11. Le Marais

Some say that the Eiffel Tower is the most Parisian thing on Earth, other say it's Saint-Germain-des-Près, I say it is a neighborhood called Le Marais. Growing up in Paris, in an area that was far from Le Marais, I always felt that it was one of the rare places in the city that even Parisian people fantasize about.

Famous for being both the Jewish and the gay neighborhood, the Marais is the best place to walk, eat, drink and shop. A lifetime wouldn't be enough to discover all its treasures, but you should still try the get the most of it during your stay. Whether you are in the mood for the best falafel in town rue des Rosiers, designers clothes or furniture rue du Roi de Sicile, or to have a drink or two rue du Temple, you won't be disappointed. It is also the best place to find vintage shops and finally get that leather jacket you have been dreaming of for a cheap price. I advise you to take the public transports to get there, as you will need all your energy for the endless walk awaiting you!

12. Rue Sainte-Anne

A must-go for Japanese food lovers! This discrete street located moments from the Palais Royal and the Opera will not provide you with the most French dishes ever, but it is definitely worth going.

You will be able to find sushi of course, but most importantly, the street has several traditional Japanese restaurants that serve delicious udon and other classic Japanese wonders. In a very authentic atmosphere, fill your stomach before you return to the busy Parisian streets. How to choose between all the places in the streets? As a rule of thumb, go for the one with the longest queue. Not a pleasant thing to hear, but it'll be worth every second spent waiting.

A very personal tip from myself to all admirers of the French actress Eva Green: one of the restaurant's door has a review from a magazine taped on the window, featuring a photo of her.

Lastly, if you are in the mood for cooking or if you are simply curious, have a look inside of the Korean Market at the end of the street. I bet you that you won't be able to leave with empty hands!

13. Rue Mouffetard

In the 5th arrondissement, there is a tiny yet quite long street that every Parisian has heard of, most having been there quite a few times.

Rue Mouffetard is a great compromise between touristic and authentic, as it is close to French universities and therefore attracts many students, but it is famous enough to have most menus translated in English. The street can get a bit crowded at night and is the perfect spot for an endless party journey. If you feel like having a look but not drinking until late, you can walk the street in the afternoon, when it is much quieter, and have lunch there. I recommend the little Italian, the prices are cheap and the serving portions, big.

You will also find some small shops selling gifts, vintage music CDs and a charming square with a few restaurants and bars, for a moment in the sun. From there you can go down the street to the Place Monge and then walk to the Jardin des Plantes, the ideal spot to have a walk and an ice-cream.

14. Free Your Inner Geek

Passionate about board games and yet tired of drinking beer and eating onion rings in pubs? Paris has the right place for you. Split across three floors and a small outside terrace, Le Dernier Bar Avant la Fin du Monde – The Last Bar Before the End of the World – is a must-go to enjoy a great dinner with friends and spend the nights trying all the games you want. With its shelf breaking under a pile of boxes, the only issue will be to choose the perfect one for you. If you cannot find the rules in English, just ask one of the waiters! They will be happy to explain you how to play any game.

Games are not the only plus of this surrealistic place in the heart of the Châtelet neighborhood. The menu changes often and features many original and varied dishes, some even suitable for vegans! You will have to hurry to enjoy the short happy hour, but the cocktails are worth it. Creative, with named inspired by the world of videogame culture, these wonders will make it hard for you to focus on your game. Since the terrace is quite small, I advise coming early in the evening if you want to get a seat there.

One last thing: when visiting the place, say hello to the E.T doll for me!

15. Be Romantic

Paris is a **very** romantic city. Everyone knows it, but I can prove it.

The Musée de la Vie Romantique is one of the most charming places I have come across during all these years living in the French capital. Located very close to Montmartre – another hugely endearing place in the city – it consists of a two-floor hotel particulier. The museum being relatively small, you won't have time to get bored going through the exhibition!

Art put aside, I consider the best thing about the Musée de la Vie Romantique to be its quiet little garden. In the spring and in the summer, you will have the privilege of enjoying a drink surrounded by blossoming flowers.

Perfect for a date or an inspired discussion about arts and...love.

16. Go Green And Trendy, Go To La Recyclerie

Going to La Recyclerie for your Sunday brunch is a Parisian thing to do, and it will enable you to discover an area that doesn't attract many tourists: La Porte de Clignancourt. Located next to the underground station, its large building overlooks the Boulevard Ornano.

Based on the idea that you should not throw anything away, this hybrid place offers various activities and a brunch cooked with sustainably grown products. If there is enough room inside for you and your friends to enjoy your meal, the best thing about la Recyclerie is its garden.

Going down the stairs, you will find a quiet outside space to work, drink a beer or simply enjoy the sun. If you like animals, don't miss out on the urban farm!

17. Le 104

Located in the Parisian North East, which in Parisian words means "authentic", the 104 is a great place to spend the afternoon if you want to combine chilling and cultural sightseeing.

A shelter to young performance artists who are using its huge space to practice, but also a great exhibition place, you will both see innovative and independent works of art while truly immersing yourself in the Parisian artistic life.

Whether you feel like grabbing a bite, having a proper lunch off the beaten tracks or spending time immersed in an artistic vibe, the 104 is the right place to go. You can let your children and yourself run around with no one to stop you, or just enjoy watching dancers practice. For a few hours, you are completely free.

18. Île De La Cité

As you might already know, the famous church Notre-Dame de Paris, one of Paris' most important monuments, is situated on an island. This little island is called Île de La Cité.

It would be a lie to say that Parisians go there every day, however, I wouldn't advise passing on this one. As a kid I remember long walks in the sun with my family, exploring this timeless and lively neighbourhood.

After a few photos/selfies in front of the church with all the other visitors, take a moment to walk for an hour on the Île de la Cité, enjoying the ancient architecture, the river and the artisanal ice-cream by Bertillon, said to be the best ice-cream in town.

19. Shopping Doesn't Rime With Galeries Lafayette

Paris is the city of love, and certainly the city of love for shopping.

You hear the name of the city and you think of Champs Elysées, Galeries Lafayette, or even Le Bon Marché. All these famous names are perfectly valid places to go shopping, but don't cry if you see your beautiful new dress on five other people in the streets - in Paris or anywhere else in the world. It doesn't have to be like this. Paris is full of streets to shop for unique designer pieces for all budgets.

Have a look Rue du Roi de Sicile in Le Marais, but not only. Everywhere in the city, open your eyes for small shops: in the 9th arrondissement around Pigalle, and in the 2nd arrondissement next to the street Etienne Marcel, you will find many.

If you really want to find your favourite brands, go to

the Beaugrenelle area. Same shops, way fewer people.

20. Green Areas

Paris is a big city, but it features some peaceful green areas. You can have a walk through the Jardin du Luxembourg - Luxembourg garden, in the iconic Saint-Germains-des-Près, which used to be the intellectual centre of Paris. If you are staying more in the North of Paris - on the Right Bank - you can have a little picnic in the Parc Monceau. Parc Monceau is small and rather charming, but avoid it at all cost on weekends, Wednesdays and times around 4 p.m, unless you enjoy sharing your personal space with a hundred children and their nannies.

My personal favorite park in Paris is the Parc des Buttes Chaumont. This one is huge, which gives you plenty of space to walk and to rest afterwards. Most of all, this park is way more immersive than the others and you could easily forget that you are in a busy city. Take an afternoon to have lunch on the grass there and read a book in the sun. Don't forget to

walk to the top of the hill and have a look at the view over

Paris!

When good Americans die, they go to Paris.

Oscar Wilde

Albane Linyer

21. The Parisian Mosque

Finally, a great place to enjoy winter in Paris! There is indeed nothing more comforting than an afternoon at the Parisian Mosque when the temperatures go down.

The place is located just next to the Jardin des Plantes and to the Arabic World Institute and its architecture is a wonder.

Still, are you going to spend the afternoon just looking at it? I recommend not to. What you can do instead, is go to the hammam and spend the day enjoying the steam, scrubbing and purifying your body while exchanging the latest gossips.

You will leave the place feeling as soft and relaxed as a new-born. If you want to keep the feeling a little longer before going home, have a delicious glass of fresh mint tea, either on the inside or the outside terrace, and why not add an Arabic pastry?

As the place has different days for men and women, you

should rather go with a friend than as a couple!

22. Parisian Terraces

Paris, its restaurants, its endless shopping opportunities, and most importantly its terraces! No other city has this obsession for terraces. With the first rays of the sun, you'll see armies of Parisians rushing to be the first on their favorite spot. Do not leave Paris without drinking your coffee in the sun, even if it's freezing. And since Paris has raised the concept of terrace to a proper art, here are some of the most interesting ones, suited for all budgets.

If you are willing to spend some money, don't miss the Ralph's, Ralph Lauren's restaurant. Its hidden courtyard on the boulevard Saint-Germain is as glamorous and sophisticated as the quality of food.

For something cheaper, have a drink at the Auteuil Brasserie, that has both a rooftop and a terrace. On the same price range, try Marcello, Italian restaurant of the 6th arrondissement for a tasty meal in a unique place - I won't tell you more about it.

Finally, whether it's time for breakfast, lunch or a drink, don't miss the famous Hotel Amour in the North of Paris. The inside patio filled with plants is a great spot to relax before some drinks in Pigalle. Fun fact: behind a romantic name, Hotel Amour used to be a hotel in which you could book a room for as short as one hour. Naughty!

23. Parisian Rooftops

In a big city, the heights are priceless to escape the noise and the crowd. Since it is hard to spot great rooftops when walking in the streets, here are two for those craving a breath-taking view over the capital, or just the privilege of being above everyone else.

If you are willing to pay what it takes for high-quality meals on the chic Avenue Montaigne, the Maison Blanche is the right place for you.

If you are more of a party animal on a budget, the Point Ephemere, great party venue in Jaurès, 19th arrondissement, has one of the best summer rooftops to enjoy a cold beer overlooking the canal. Enjoy music, French party people and then go down to the club part and stay until morning!

24. Tips For Animal Owners

Taking your animal with you on holidays is a great adventure, but can happen to be a little complicated when you don't know the city. Restaurants that won't allow your dog, parks that will forbid access, a lot can go wrong as you go for a walk.

In Paris, supermarkets will usually not allow you to take your dog with you. However, if you want to sit at a terrace, it is most likely that your friend will be welcome. If you need to take your dog out, there are some places that should be enjoyable for you and for them.

Le Parc des Buttes-Chaumont, one of the biggest parks in Paris, allows dogs. So does the Ranelagh, in the 16th arrondissement. The Parc Monceau also allows dogs, but only in the alleys. You and your dog will find new friends to meet on the Halles lawns, in the centre.

Now you know where to take your furry friend when

they are part of the journey!

25. Temples Of Contemporary Art

Museums lovers, be ready! Paris has enough addresses to keep you busy every hour of your stay.

For those eager to see some contemporary art, run to the famous and yet never boring Centre Georges Pompidou. Located in the Beaubourg area, the museum is surrounded by cafes, restaurants and street artists. If you are on a budget and lucky enough to find an available seat, go have a drink at the bar Les Fontaines afterwards. Cheap prices, but everyone knows it and after 5 p.m it is a miracle to find a place to sit!

Another home to contemporary art and a very interesting place in itself, le Palais de Tokyo. In the 16th arrondissement so a bit further west to the centre, the building never ceases to amaze me. In addition to the exhibition spaces, have a look at the shop that often has funny gadgets and unusual objects,

46

and at the restaurant. If the weather allows it, you can chill on its beautiful terrace.

Try and have look at what's happening at Le Grand Palais. The building is every year home to the Contemporary Art Fair, and in the summer, it often hosts events such as concerts, exhibitions and movie nights.

When you have had enough of paintings, installations, and performances, go and see some photos at the European House of Photography!

26. Explore Paris's Most Special Little Museums

The Louvre is extraordinary, the Palais de Tokyo is a fantastic place to see contemporary art, but are all museums only meant to expose works of art? I say they're not, and Paris is the living proof of it. Hidden and poorly known by most of native Parisians and even more by tourists, the city hides in its streets, small yet fascinating museums. I would

47

have myself never found out about them if my grandmother hadn't had a passion for taking me to these unusual places on my free Wednesdays.

Did you know there was a Museum of Bread and Bakery? Not very surprising, but quite unexpected. Another important one is the Museum of Fairground Arts - Musée des Arts Forains. Located in the Bercy neighbourhood, the museum is entirely about leisure, having fun and entertainment. Not only will you be able to see ancient objects from the world of the performing arts, but there are also many interactive activities available, such as vintage rides! A must-go if you have children with you or if you are still fascinated by the world of fun-fairs and keen on having a museum experience off the beaten tracks.

My personal favourite of Paris' alternative museums is the Museum of Counterfeit - Musée de la Contrefaçon. A very entertaining exhibition around iconic brands and fake products.

Ask around, there are many small museums worth a visit!

27. Have A Break, Have A Hot Chocolate

One of my favourite things to do is spending a day walking in Le Marais with someone I care about. Shopping or window-shopping for hours in the small streets, being amazed by people's outfits, discovering new places.

After hours walking, we often need a break and preferably a cheap one - Le Marais being the most threatening place in Paris for your wallet.

When it's cold outside, I never miss an occasion to seek shelter in the small Piment Cafe. Not only does the place have a warm setting, but it serves the very best hot chocolate I've ever had, for a reasonable price.

28. Traditional French Food In A "Brasserie"

Equivalent to the English pub or the American dinner, a "brasserie" is the typical place for French people to have lunch or dinner. Perfect mix of price and quality, the brasserie has in reliability what it lacks in originality. Nothing experimental, nothing grandiose but well-made French food, good cheese and good wine.

The kind of typical food you will find there - I don't advise any vegans to pass the door - steak with pepper sauce, foie gras, grilled salmon, beef tartare.

My personal favourite place to have traditional French food - best tartare and fries I have ever had, and I tried many places - is the Bistrot des Halles. Just next to the huge shopping mall, in a quieter street, get there early to get a table.

To find a brasserie restaurant, just have a walk. Usually, the word "brasserie" will be written on the windows.

29. Le Relais De l'Entrecôte

Nowadays, you can find restaurants called l'Entrecôte in many cities in the world. However, I have tried some of them and the test has confirmed my original belief: the only ones that matter are in Paris.

There are three restaurants Le Relais de L'Entrecôte in Paris, so you can choose whichever is close to where you stay.

The secret of having a queue every day for lunch and dinner lies in the recipe: one meal fits all, contre-filet cut of sirloin served with a special secret sauce, and of course the incredible homemade fries. The atmosphere is typical old Paris, warm and welcoming. The waitresses are famous for being exceptionally efficient, and that is for a reason: they have shares in the restaurant and care about it as if it were their own. If you still have room for a desert, have a go at the chocolate profiteroles - perfection.

30. Treat You Inner Meat Lover

French people love meat, and they prove it by offering the best quality in their restaurants. Louchebem is a very old French restaurant specialised in meat. A family business in the busy Chatelet area, the place has built its reputation on the quality of the food.

But there is more to Louchebem than good meat, there is the famous rôtisseur plate - l'assiette du rôtisseur. L'assiette du rôtisseur is a plate that contains three kinds of meat - beef, ham, and lamb. Fresh meat that you get All you can eat. Yes, you read well. All. You. Can. Eat. The best thing is that if you'd rather have only one of these kinds on your plate, you can ask for it, and the formula will remain All you can eat.

To sum it up, there is no better address for a huge meat craving. Booking is advised since the restaurant is full most of the time.

We'll always have Paris.

Humphrey Bogart

- Casablanca

Albane Linyer

31. Where to Take a Fish-Lover

After a couple of tips on where to eat fabulous meat in Paris, here's the place where you want to go to have awesome fish.

La Marée Jeanne offers a very creative menu, amazing original creations and homemade bread and butter. Located next to the busy Montorgeuil street, the restaurant is one of my favourite places to have dinner in Paris. The prices are not too high, it is a trendy little place. Call in advance to make sure you'll get a table!

Rather go with a friend than as a couple, as the chatty atmosphere and the small tables don't make for a very romantic scenery. Less hand holding, more food testing!

If the restaurant is full and you still feel like fish, walk three more minutes and have a try at La Cevicheria. The specialty is - as you might have guessed - ceviche, which is raw fish and seasoning. The place has an outside space and gathers trendy Parisians of all generations. The ceviche is fresh and tasty, but the serving portions are be a bit small if you have an appetite. Make sure you have enough on your plate by sharing a side with your friends!

32. How To Tip In Paris

Tipping around the world requires a specific knowledge of the country and its inhabitants. Parisians are considered to be terrible at it, but this might just be because our tipping culture is a bit different from others.

However, tipping is very important if you don't want to offend your waiter or waitress. In France, the waiters are not paid with the tips money, nor is the tip included in the bill.

So how do you tip in Paris? Obviously, it depends on the restaurant. Going to an expensive restaurant forces you to tip more, if you don't want to seem rude.

Leave 1 to 15 euros, according to your satisfaction and to the place's standards.

33. Take A Walk Alongside The Canal St Martin

I have told you about bikes, buses, taxis, vintage cars, but what if you could simply use...your feet?

There are great walks to do in Paris, but this one is one of the longest and will allow you to discover Paris in all its beauty. Beautiful on a cold or a sunny day, but of course try to avoid the rain. I recommend you to finish with the 19th arrondissement and to have a drink at the bar Point Ephemere or at La Rotonde de Salingrad to celebrate and rest your legs!

You can also enjoy the path on your skateboard ! And if you are not tired by the time you arrive in Stalingrad, why not walk more to the Parc de la Villette, a huge outdoor space where you will find the Cité de la Science.

34. Best Place To Buy Yourself Or Your Beloved One A Present

Paris, like most cities in our modern world, has a great number of sex shops, and most of them are everything but…sexy. Impersonal spaces, a weird vibe, and a cruel lack of any glamour, most shops will probably make you want to leave immediatly.

What a shame, when there are so many things that you could experiment alone or as a couple! Believe it or not, Paris has a place dedicated to physical love that is clean, sexy and, I have to say, quite adorable. Its name: Le Passage du Désir.

There are a few shops in Paris, three located around the 1st and the 4th arrondissement. You will find funny postcards, playful gadgets, books, anything to have fun with. For adults only, but in a charming way.

35. Bargain At The St Ouen Flea Market

Welcome to the biggest Flea Market in the world! The St Ouen Flea Market is spread across 6 hectares, so be ready to be on your feet for a while!

From antique furniture to clothes and books, you can find about anything vintage there. If you feel ready to bargain in French, don't be afraid. However, it can be the perfect occasion to ask some locals to spend the day together and benefit from their mother tongue! Some companies also offer tours with a French guide, so you can learn about the place and get the best prices all at once.

So wake-up early to find the best items for the cheapest price and spend a thrilling day!

One warning: as always in crowded places, take care of your personal belongings.

36. Visit Edith Piaf and Jim Morrison

If you haven't had the occasion to meet your idols before they passed away, you might get a second chance in Paris. The Père Lachaise cemetery is one of Paris' special spots that you will find in no other city.

Whether you are visiting Oscar Wilde, Marcel Proust or Frederic Chopin, some of the most famous and admired personalities of all times will be waiting there for you...forever.

A walk through the cemetery is the occasion to see tombstones of some of the greatest artists that have ever lived but also to enjoy a moment aside from the noise and the rush of the city.

A moment to think, to remember and to look forward.

37. Have a Vintage Ride on The Champs Elysées

France wouldn't be France without its iconic car, the Deux Chevaux, Citroen2CV. Seen in many movies, driven by famous actors, it has even made an appearance in an episode of the animated show South Park.

The Deux Chevaux is both a French cliché and a worldwide reference when it comes to vintage cars.

What if I said you could combine both visiting the city and experimenting a ride on one of these famous beauties? Some companies offer guided tours of the capital in the car with a guide. A tour both private and unconventional, that won't give you the most typical Parisian experience but most likely an unforgettable one!

Have a look online to find the tour that suits you the best.

38. Go to The Theatre

Paris is the kind of city that has a great cultural life: within the city, one could say that a new play is showing every day.

For those who speak French you can choose between the classic yet astonishing Comédie Française, La Gaieté Lyrique, Théâtre de l'Odéon and so on. Sky is the limit and every theatre emanates a different charm.

For those who don't, don't believe French theatre is not accessible to you. The company Theatre in Paris allows you to see classical French plays in French with English subtitles. A way to feel Parisian and enjoy the text the way it was written, while being able to follow the story!

My ultimate must-see, that luckily benefits from these subtitles, is the French play Cyrano de Bergerac, written by Edmond Rostand.

39. Spend a Moment...In the Sky

A romantic or simply impressive thing to do in Paris is going to the Planetarium. In its beautiful space, you will be able to choose between different immersive shows to get the best sky experiment. The visual quality is provided by an ultra-modern equipment, the Planetarium being one of the only two spots in the world to have it.

The Planetarium is in the Cité de la Science, an immense building dedicated to science and explaining, located in the Parisian East. An afternoon would not be enough to reveal all the place's wonders. You will also find interactive spaces for children, so feel free to bring the whole family! And if it is sunny outside, bring your lunch to eat on the grass, in the huge Parc de la Villette. The place is also accessible skating or cycling, thanks to the cycling track that starts from Jaurès tube station.

40. Go On A Safari (Personal Car Needed)

Ok, a safari might not be the main reason you've come to France. Still, if you are in town for a while and your children are getting tired of museums, why not take them out for a bit of fresh air?

One of the great things about Paris is also that going outside of Paris is quite easy and adds more potential activities. There is Disneyland, of course, but unless it is winter or you are lucky enough to go on a Tuesday outside of the usual holiday times, you're mostly going to remember the very long queuing lines.

If you are looking for something a bit more unusual, there is the safari zoo of Thoiry. In your own car, drive among the wild animals in perfect safety. Their website has an English version on which you can book tickets and find more information!

Paris is always a good idea.

Audrey Hepburn - *Sabrina*

Albane Linyer

41. Take Your Kids For A Ride In A Park!

I can probably speak for most of the children raised in Paris by saying this: Le Jardin d'Acclimatation is a **lot** of fun. I have been there many times as a child, and even as a teenager, because why would you grow out of fun?

In the very West of Paris, in a huge green area, you will find this little paradise that features a theme park and a zoo. Want your kids to enjoy a ride, shoot some cans to win prizes and be amazed at the sight of peacocks chilling on the grass? Le Jardin d'Acclimatation is the place to go. You can spend the day walking in the park, reading or running after the little ones already high on ice-cream and fun.

Bear in mind that there are no roller coasters, to avoid disappointing the most adventurous members of the family.

42. Montmartre And Its Gardens

Paris's beauty lies in unexpected places that you would never go to unless someone has told you about them. Did you even know Montmartre had vineyards that still produce grapes for wine today? Or that there is a small statue of Dalida on the Dalida square, right next to these same vineyards?

Montmartre still has so many secrets that you will discover most of them by accident. This is what happened to me with the Montmartre Museum and the Renoir Gardens. On the Montmartre hill, the museum located in Montmartre is all about…Montmartre.

With its permanent exhibition, you will be able to discover the history of the village, of its vineyards and when Montmartre officially became part of Paris.

The best thing about the place is that the outside is even more beautiful than the inside! Indeed, three gardens, the

68

Renoir Gardens surround the place and overlook Montmartre, the vineyards and the northern part of Paris. Romantic, cultural and Parisian to the core.

43. Go Underground For A Cocktail

A spot Parisians know for deserving its reputation is the Beef Club's Ballroom. The Beef Club is a well-known restaurant, the Ballroom is its bar. After a steak and a glass of red wine, go treat yourself with a high-quality cocktail.

Why going underground? Because the magic happens below the ground. Once you have reached its door, the bar offers the most intimate atmosphere, with a small bar featuring the crème de la crème of alcohols. Let the magicians behind the counter prepare a cocktail just according to your taste, or one of their latest creations.

No gin tonics or tequila sunrises here, all the cocktails are originals. In this timeless space, relax and get to know the other privileged members of the club. Signature cocktails, a

speak-easy atmosphere and you're set for an unforgettable

experience.

44. Go and Listen to Some French Music in A Basement

It does sound like a weird idea, but is there a better way

to get the French touch than going to a bar that plays mostly

French vintage music? Probably not.

Chai Antoine is ideally located on a quiet street, it is

unlikely that you would ever pass the door without knowing

precisely where you are going. If you want to feel special in a

small place with great atmosphere and French people

enjoying the best hits their country has brought to the world,

Chai Antoine is the place to spend the night.

If you don't want to be standing all night, you can book

a table for you and your friends, either in the dancing or the smoking area and enjoy the night and a seat. The cosiness of the space will most likely lead you to make some new friends.

When you engage conversation, don't forget what I've told you about sentences to avoid!

45. Find A Cheap Beer...Thanks To Your Phone

What if you could instantly see every bar in the area and the price of their pint of beer, during and after the happy hour? As the saying goes: there's an app for that.

All Parisian students and young professionals have used this app once in their lives and the name is simple to remember: MrGoodBeer.

I would advise using the app to find an area with a few bars, so if one is full, you can try the next one. As of experience, walking 20 minutes to get the cheapest beer and not finding a seat can be quite infuriating. Now, cheers to traveling and to cheap beer!

Remember that even though apps and phones are useful to finding your way in a foreign city, asking a local will make your experience richer and will force you to look around instead of staring at your screen.

46. What Do Parisian Women Keep in Their Purses?

A lot has been said about Paris, and almost as much has been said about French women. Most beautiful in the world, thinnest in Europe; true or not, these beliefs have built the image of a chic, friendly and free-minded creature.

I can't tell you who French women really are, but some say that looking in a woman's purse, in addition to being very rude, will tell you everything about her.

First of all, you should know that French women carry their lipstick everywhere. They don't use much makeup in everyday life, so this little stick is enough to look perfect in every situation.

Cash, because like in ancient times, you often need it to pay in Paris.

A book, because what do you do in the tube or waiting for a friend at the bar?

And a notebook. A notebook in your bag allows you to draw and take notes during the whole day. Paris is inspiring and iPhone batteries die fast. Beware: in Paris, it is quite hard to find somewhere to plug your phone.

This tip is less a list of things you must have in your bag than a general observation of the Parisian lifestyle.

As for what **you** should carry with you while visiting Paris, I will also suggest something: unless you are **really** good at taking pictures and a camera will make the difference, use your phone. Faster to Instagram, Snapchat, and way lighter. Plus, you will look less like a tourist.

47. Where To Go If You Need To Work

Spending a wonderful time, enjoying your holidays? It might not last. Your boss is never too far, and we all recognise that inner panic attack you get at the sight of a professional email, when you were just trying to send your latest selfies to your parents. Of course you need to answer, and of course you don't want to go all the way back to your hotel/hostel/Airbnb and lock yourself away from this new city.

It took me years to learn how to face that kind of situation. When you need silence to focus, working in most coffee places is a no-go. People chat, drink, which makes it impossible to get anything done. Thanks to a friend, I have

74

finally found the perfect shelter for my brain cells and my professional self: the Anticafé. There are five in Paris, so you should be able to find one in your area. The concept is rather simple: you pay per hour and you can have as many drinks - non-alcoholic – and snacks as you like. High-speed Wi-Fi and board games, you will find everything you need for a productive afternoon followed by a bit of chilling!

48. What To Bring Back From Paris

As soon as you will pass your doorstep, you're going to get the one and only question, and it won't be "How was it?". People will ask you what you brought them from your trip.

If you don't want to find yourself looking at your feet, realising that you even forgot to buy an Eiffel Tower key ring, here are some really French stuff you could bring back home.

First and best: French wine. To get a good wine for a

reasonable price, I recommend to try a shop called Nicolas. They have stores almost everywhere in Paris and have a lot of choice. Ask for a good "vin de table" and you cannot go wrong.

Another French specialty that travels well is the saucisson, the French dried sausage. Delicious cut in thin slices, served with a glass of wine and some olives. Try a local butchery, or even a supermarket butchery, they should have what you are looking for.

Foie gras should also please everyone. You can find some at a local butchery. If you are traveling for a long time, make sure the product is vacuum-packed, so it stays in perfect condition until it gets home.

Finally, if you want something that nobody can eat, you can bring friends and family a gift from Le Slip Français. All the clothes are 100% made in France, great quality and the design is flawless. The brand has three shops in Paris and the store itself is worth the visit!

So now you know what to bring home, but only if they deserve it!

49. Come Again

Because even if you are a superhero and have managed to find time to experience everything listed in that guide, I am sorry and glad to tell you that there is still **a lot** to see in Paris.

Some cities are famous for one monument, for one great church, but Paris is constantly moving and changing. That is why I keep on coming back myself every time I get the occasion! There is always a new spot, a new restaurant, a street that I had never heard of.

These are some clues for you to see the amazing things that make Paris the city in the world I love the most. It is now your turn to find out more!

50. To Prepare Your Journey, Watch Movies

Paris is a very photogenic city and many directors have made it almost a character in their films. To have a look at the city before you visit it, here are some classics that should make you look even more forward to your trip!

Agnès Warda is one of the only women directors of the French Nouvelle Vague. She has directed *Cléo de 5 à 7* (*Cleo from 5 to 7*), 1962, a film that follows a woman, Cleo, during an hour and a half journey across the capital. This realistic tale is both an exploration of the city and of the French Nouvelle Vague's particular language.

Paris I love you is a two-hour compilation movie featuring 20 short movies from famous directors such as the Coen brothers and Gus Van Sant. A poem in twenty parts, a rich analysis of Paris and its neighbourhoods that I highly recommend watching to fall in love with the city and cinema all over again.

More recently, Woody Allen has dedicated *Midnight in Paris* to the mythic French capital, at the time of Hemingway and glitters.

There are many ways to travel for the first time without - yet - leaving your couch.

Albane Linyer

Top Reasons to Book A Trip To Paris

- **Sightseeing**: Paris has many incredible monuments that you want to have seen in your life!

- **The food**: a lifetime wouldn't be enough to try all these delicious Parisian restaurants.

- **Paris**: every minute feels like being in a movie, and that is priceless.

Albane Linyer

> TOURIST

GREATER THAN A TOURIST

Visit GreaterThanATourist.com
http://GreaterThanATourist.com

Sign up for the Greater Than a Tourist Newsletter
http://eepurl.com/cxspyf

Follow us on Facebook:
https://www.facebook.com/GreaterThanATourist

Follow us on Pinterest:
http://pinterest.com/GreaterThanATourist

Follow us on Instagram:
http://Instagram.com/GreaterThanATourist

Albane Linyer

> TOURIST

GREATER THAN A TOURIST

Please leave your honest review of this book on Amazon and Goodreads. Thank you.

We appreciate your positive and negative feedback as we try to provide tourist guidance in their next trip from a local.

> TOURIST

GREATER THAN A TOURIST

Our Story

Traveling is a passion of the "Greater than a Tourist" series creator. Lisa studied abroad in college, and for their honeymoon Lisa and her husband toured Europe. During her travels to Malta, an older man tried to give her some advice based on his own experience living on the island since he was a young boy. She was not sure if she should talk to the stranger but was interested in his advice. When traveling to some places she was wary to talk to locals because she was afraid that they weren't being genuine. Through her travels, Lisa learned how much locals had to share with tourists. Lisa created the "Greater Than a Tourist" book series to help connect people with locals. A topic that locals are very passionate about sharing.

Albane Linyer

> TOURIST

GREATER THAN A TOURIST

Notes

Made in the USA
Lexington, KY
28 December 2017